BASKETBALL'S PRINCETON-STYLE OFFENSE

A Simplified Approach for High School Coaches

W0008693

Derek Sheridan

Wish Publishing
Terre Haute, Indiana
www.wishpublishing.com

Basketball's Princeton-Style Offense: A Simplified Approach for High School Students © 2008 Derek Sheridan

All rights reserved under International and Pan-American Copyright Conventions

No part of this book may be reproduced, stored in a data base or other retrieval system, or transmitted in any form, by any means, including mechanical, photocopy, recording or otherwise, without the prior written permission of the publisher.

Library of Congress Control Number: 2008931254

Edited by Heather Lowhorn

Editorial assistance provided by Dorothy Chambers

Cover designed by Phil Velikan

Printed in the United States of America

10 9 8 7 6 5 4 3 2 1

Published in the United States by Equilibrium Books, A Division of Wish Publishing, P.O. Box 10337, Terre Haute, IN 47801, USA, www.wishpublishing.com

*To my wife, Stephanie, and my parents and grandparents
who have supported me through the good and bad alike.*

Table of Contents

Introduction

The simplified Princeton offense is a style that is a good fit for high school teams that do not have a great deal of height and/or players who can create their own shots. This book breaks down the elements of the Princeton offense and explains it in simple terms and clear diagrams. I used this offense with my own high school teams and even started running limited versions of this offense at the sixth- and seventh-grade levels.

Many people believe the Princeton offense is too complicated, and, admittedly, it took some time to learn how this offense worked. I had been fascinated by it for several years, but there were no teaching tapes or books available. I learned by watching countless hours of games that I had taped off the television. I also made contact with a school that ran the offense and had them send me several tapes. Over the years, I accumulated almost 70 tapes. But once I cracked the code, it became apparent that the Princeton-style offense is no more difficult to learn than any standard motion offense. I just had to link the parts to the whole and find out what keyed certain movements. And after you have read this book, I hope you find that the Princeton offense is not so complicated, too.

If I were to try to thank all of the people who helped me in my education of this offense, I would most certainly forget someone. So I will give you the name of the person who spent the most time in helping me with those first few steps. Coach Jerry O'Brien from Gibson Southern High School in southern Indiana was very gracious and instrumental in helping me start to see the parts, rather than the whole. Even when I was interrupting his meal or calling him at an obscenely late hour, he was never short or impatient with me. Coach O'Brien is a true coach's coach. I might add that, in my opinion, his teams run this offense better than anyone else at the high school and middle school levels.

I would also be remiss if I didn't mention Jack Gabor, Nino Muffeletto, Paul Patterson, Flava Sirk, Rick Van Matre, Beaver Marceneck, Dean Foster, Jim McDonald, Tom Johnson, Jim Burson and Jim Irwin. All of these coaches ran programs that consistently beat teams who had superior talent. I took something from each of them and will forever be thankful for their mentorship. If you ever aspire to learn more about shooting the basketball, work Dick Baumgartner's shooting camp in Richmond, Indiana. He is the best teacher of shooting that I have ever been around.

I also need to thank my college coach, Steve Platt. How he ever won with our teams is still a mystery to me. We beat teams that we had no business competing with. Although it was not with this offense, he taught me the importance of discipline, hard work and practicing with a purpose. Coach was about as hard-nosed as they come, and that attitude most definitely rubbed off on us. After playing for Coach Platt I had intangibles and core values ingrained within me that I still live my life by today.

I would also like to thank Mrs. Shauna Bohlmann, one of our high school English teachers. Mrs. Bohlman took the time to edit this book for me.

Chapter 1
Myths about the Princeton Offense

Many coaches reject the Princeton offense, also called the backdoor offense, because of myths they have heard about this style of play. For example, some coaches believe that to use the Princeton offense you must have unusually intelligent players in your program. Others think it is only a "slow down" offense. And other coaches believe it is an antiquated offense that takes too long to teach.

Obviously, I don't accept those myths as true. Many of the players that I had running this offense were average students. Unselfishness is more important than brains, a player's "I will" is more important than his "I.Q." It is not a "slow down" offense. Many teams, including one of mine, have run a secondary break into the flow of the offense. Princeton, Georgetown and N.C. State have also gotten the ball down the sideline in an attempt to get early offense initiated.

It does take time to teach this, especially during the first year. But so did motion when we taught it. Once you have a foundation built at the lower levels and your current high school teams are running it, the teaching becomes less time consuming. And I contend that players have just as much freedom, if not more, to make reads in this offensive system as they would or do when executing in any motion offense.

My own teams ran this offense because it fit our personnel. We lacked a dominant post player, and we didn't have much height. We had undersized post players who were able to step away from the basket and make passes to cutters and shoot perimeter shots. Our perimeter players were best at shooting spot-up shots and not having to create their own shots.

The Princeton offense allowed us to shorten the game, and it put pressure on our opponents. They had to spend more time preparing to play against our offense. It allowed us to compete against teams who played hard denial defense, because this offense has all types of pressure releases.

Basketball's Princeton-Style Offense

Our players also needed structure, and the Princeton offense provided that. It provided us with very specific practice objectives and breakdown drills.

The Princeton offense, like all other styles of offensive play, does have drawbacks. When you first begin teaching it you will be criticized by the experts in the stands and by players who think they are all-stars. Both the coaches and the players will need lots of patience. It can be difficult to come from behind in a game with this offense, too. But the positives outweigh the negatives, and you won't be sorry you took the time to learn the Princeton offense.

Chapter 2
General Thoughts and Application Rules

Before we jump into the nuts and bolts of the Princeton offense, I want to offer some general points that may help you learn and teachthis style of play. Some of these points you may understand immediately, and some you might not grasp until you are deeper into the offense. But here are the points your players should know up front:

1. The post player is the only true "position" player. Fundamentally sound players are more important than positions.

2. The player should watch the person in front of him; he tells the player what to do.

3. The player should read the defense before he makes his move. For most situations, the player involved in a play will have two options: One, the defense is overplaying; therefore the player will execute a backdoor cut. Two, the defense is sagging; therefore the player will accept a sweep from the ball handler. There is a counter for everything the defense does. Your player must be able to make a quick read when the ball is dribbled at him.

4. Players must Cut hard. They must cut all the way to the rim with the inside hand extended out. The should think "layup" on each cut. The will look for the ball twice then get out of the way.

5. The player should stand ready to shoot when off the ball. Butt down and fingers up. Players should think "layups and three-point shots," in that order.The player will occupy his man and float to open spots. If there is no answer at the backdoor, they should knock on the front.

6. Players don't dance. They are to make a read and cut hard. Once a cut is started, they should cut hard and get out of the way.

7. The player should always be ready to fill the spot above him with proper timing.

8. Players shouldn't screen the air. They must get body-on-body on all screens and be ready to step back for a shot.

9. The player will hit the cutter with a bounce pass. The quality of your player's passing will be in direct correlation to the quality of his shooting. The bounce pass is low, and it's hard to steal or deflect. Pass the ball right behind the defender's behind.

10. It's a "blue collar" offense; all five players must work together.

11. Players must dribble with a purpose.

12. Patience coupled with focus is a virtue in this system. Your players might run four sets in a single possession.

13. It's all about unselfishness, fundamental play and timing. They are the foundations for establishing the flow of the offense.

14. Keep the area below the free-throw line empty when playing against a team that is better or more athletic. Try to "out fundamental" them. Keep post defenders away from the basket.

15. Few quick hitters are used.

16. Repetition is the "mother of all learning."

17. The post player has to be a good passer. His options are S-R-P (Score - Read - Pass).

18. Players shouldn't run at the ball—greedy players run at the ball. The back cut is used to offset defensive aggressiveness.

19. Use the dribble and pass off of the dribble to keep from telegraphing passes. At the high school level, this rule will not apply to all of your players. We had some players that we told to come to a jump stop and use pass fakes rather than pass off of the dribble.

20. When a player backdoor cuts from the top of the key, he will exit out to the strong side of the floor if he was not passed the ball. When a player backdoor cuts from a wing, he will exit back out to the side from which he came.

21. A strong-side sweep equals a weak-side flare.

22. When the strong-side forward catches the ball, his first look is to feed the post.

23. When the ball is on the wing, the post has to work hard to stay in line with the ball.

24. Don't run the same phase twice in a row –think "change."

From a coach's perspective, the following are reasons to choose the Princeton offense:

1. Necessity

2. Player talent level varies

3. Negates opposition strength

4. Control

5. Offense becomes defense

From a player's perspective, the Princeton offense provides the following:

1. Confidence

2. Options

3. It's undefendable

4. Constant movement

5. Development of shooting skills

Terminology

1. Pinch post—The elbow areas.

2. Sweep—When the player with the ball runs a dribble hand-off move. He also uses his body to set a screen while sweeping. The player receiving the sweep has to pause behind the screen and read the defense.

3. Drift—When the post player sets a flare screen for another player.

4. Phases—Sets that link together to form the offenses structure.

5. Roll dribble—When the player with the ball executes a reverse spin dribble or "pearl" move with the ball.

6. Read spot—Areas that are about one foot off the pinch posts.

7. G—Guard

8. F—Forward

9. P—Post

Diagram Key

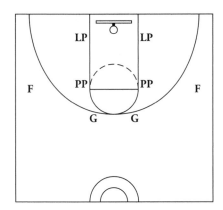 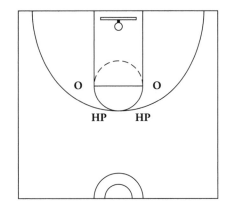

I.   PLAYER WITH THE BALL IS CIRCLED: ① ② ③ ④ ⑤

II. PASS: ─ ─ ─ ─ ─ ─ ─ ─ ─ ─ ─ ➤

III. SCREEN: ─────────────┤

IV. CUT: ────────────────➤

V.   DRIBBLE: ⌄⌄⌄⌄⌄⌄⌄➤

VI. SWEEP: ═══

VII. DEFENSIVE PLAYERS: X1 X2 X3 X4 X5

Chapter 3
Entries

How a team enters into the offense is of paramount importance. For the most part, once the strong-side forward has received the ball, everything is set. However, most good teams are going to make it hard for him to receive the ball easily. Having multiple entries will help.

The best passer and decision maker should be the strong-side forward (3-man). The first option is always to get the ball to player 3. Only reverse the ball (G-G-F) if 3 is unable to receive a pass.

If player 3 isn't open, then the team must run another entry. If at all possible, don't pass the ball to 3 if he is too high on the wing – this makes feeding the post too difficult. We position our players as follows:

1. Best ball handler
2. Best shooter and second-best ball-handler
3. Best passing forward
4. Second-best passing forward and best post-up forward
5. Best post player

    A. Can score off blocks

    B. Can score on perimeter

    C. Above-average ball handler

    D. Good passer

    E. Can read how his teammates are being guarded

        a. Closely = backdoor

        b. Loosely = sweep

Basketball's Princeton-Style Offense

We spent a lot of practice time teaching our forwards to get open on the wings.

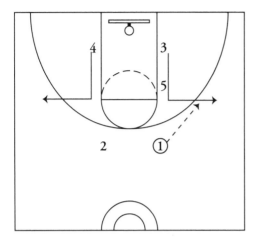

Diagram 1: L-Cuts

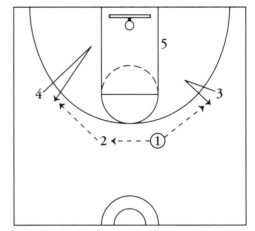

Diagram 2: V-Cuts

Guard-Forward Entry

The guard-forward entry is the most basic and most used. Player 1 gets the ball up the court and to Player 3 as soon as he can. Player 3 must execute a V-cut toward the free-throw line prior to receiving a pass. The proper timing of this move is crucial, especially when entering the ball to him during a half-court walk-up situation. As mentioned earlier, if Player 1 can get the ball up the sideline to him (as in a secondary break situation), this really makes the entry a lot easier.

Once Player 3 has the ball and has squared up to the basket, Player 1 will cut hard to the basket and exit out to the weak-side corner as quickly as he can. Player 2 cuts to the middle of the floor, standing with his behind facing the opposite sideline.

Basic Low Post Offense Alignment and G-F Entry

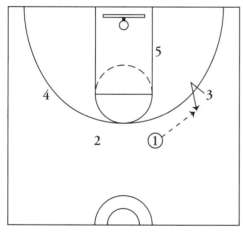

Diagram 3: G-F pass = point guard cuts through to the opposite corner.

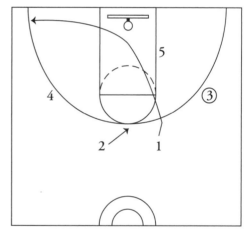

Diagram 4: The 2-guard cuts to the top of the key.

Guard-Guard or Reversal Entry

The ball is reversed to Player 2. Player 2 is looking for Player 4. Player 5 cannot cut until Player 4 has the ball, or else he will plug up the lane for backdoor cuts. Since Player 2 made the guard-forward pass, he will cut through to the opposite corner. Player 4's first move/thought is cutting to the back door. It is important to note that the 5-man has to keep his defender occupied.

Basic G-G Entry

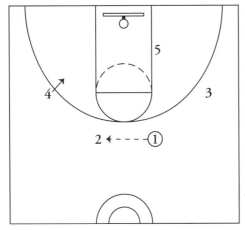

Diagram 5: Ball is reversed from G-G.

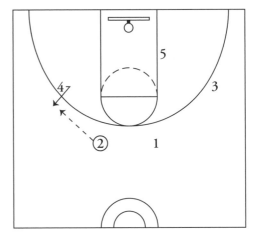

Diagram 6: Player 2G passes to strong side F.

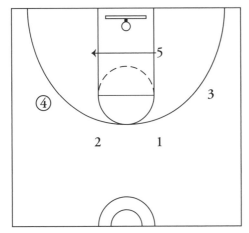

Diagram 7: The post player relocates to opposite block as soon as Player 4 catches the ball.

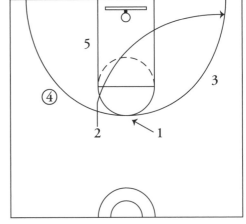

Diagram 8: Player 2G will cut through to the opposite corner (G-F pass) and Player 1 will cut to the top of the floor.

Chapter 4
Low Post Play Phases/Sets

A post feed will result in one of two actions: The passer will execute an elbow screen or forward drop. Use an elbow screen when the opposition sags defensively as an attempt to take away the backdoor cuts.

We ran the forward drop phases against teams that overplayed the passing lanes. This is something that we determined during the prior week of practice. It's simple: If player 3 feeds the post and drops to the corner, we are running a forward drop.

Elbow Screen

Upon catching the ball on the wing, the player's first look is to the post player on the low block. Begin by showing the actions of the elbow screen. The elbow screen is initiated by a G-F pass and F-P post feed.

At the conclusion of an elbow screen action, the offense will be restarted with the ball back to either the strong-side forward or to the player at the top of the key. Teach the post to skip the ball when faced with a double team coming from the weak side of the court. This is an area that is often overlooked, and one that must be practiced.

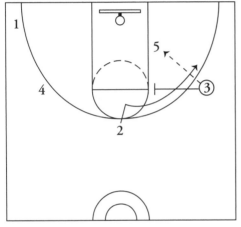

Diagram 9: Straight cut (G-F entry has already been run).

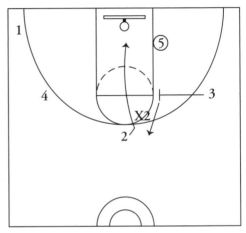

Diagram 10: Backdoor cut (defense is overplaying).

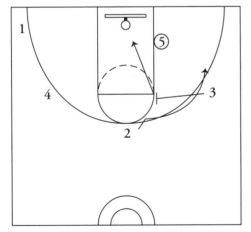

Diagram 11: Slip screen (defense is switching screens).

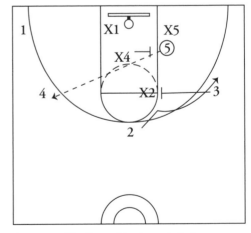

Diagram 12: Post skip (post is being doubled from the weak side).

Forward Drop

The forward drop is keyed by G-F and F-P passes. After feeding the post, either run an elbow screen action or a forward drop action. There are only two forward drop actions that my teams run: backdoor and step back, or if the post cannot make an immediate pass, the post dribble.

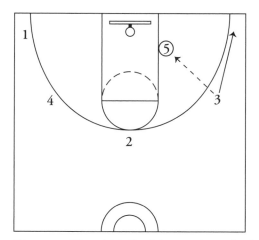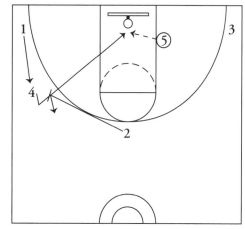

Diagrams 13 and 14: Backdoor and step back. Timing note: As soon as player 3 drops, player 2 screens for player 4.

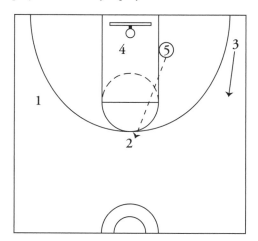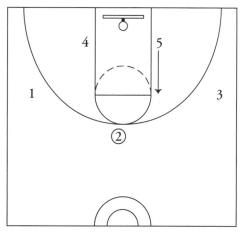

Diagrams 15: Pass mode to player 2, who is stepping back after the setting with no screen

Diagram 16: You are now ready for a drift or pinch post options.

Drift Phase

The drift phase is initiated by an F-G pass after the entry has been run. The strong-side forward catches the ball and makes two quick reads. Firstly, the post cannot be passed to. Secondly, player 2's defender is in a sagging or flat triangle defensive position; therefore, he can be passed to without interference. As soon as the post sees that an F-G pass is being made, he must cut up to the strong-side pinch post. He must cut in such a way that he gives the 2-man an option to pass to him. Ideally, he wants to make his cut as the ball is in the air, from F-G.

After the F-G pass is made, the 2-man will initiate this phase by taking a couple dribbles at the 4-man (more often than not sending him backdoor). This cut is a great backdoor option. The 4-man can sweep with player 2, but often he is being overplayed, so he cuts backdoor. The key is that player 4 has to wait until he is dribbled at and eye contact has been established between himself and player 2. The 4-man must cut behind his defender. Player 1 must sprint and fill player 4's old position. Player 1 has to get open.

Player 4 finishes his cut and waits passively for the 1-man to get the ball. As soon as player 1 catches the ball, player 4 will leg whip his defender and post up hard. This is a great opportunity for a post feed. It is important to note that the only time we ran an elbow screen or forward drop was when the 5-man was fed. With that being said, on a feed to player 4 or anyone other than player 5, the players did not run an elbow-screen action or a forward drop.

If the 4-man isn't fed, player 5 will set a drift screen on player 2's defender. Player 2 has to set his man up for this screen by taking him down toward the free-throw line. The timing of this action is keyed by the 4-man. Player 5 will not set the drift screen until the 4 man exits the low post. This gives player 2 time to set his man up for the drift action.

Coming off the drift screen, player 2 is looking for a three-point shot first and a driving opportunity second. The offense is reset by player 2 penetrating and kicking to the 3-man and then cutting (G-F pass) through to the opposite corner.

Often times, when player 2 comes off of player 5's drift screen, his defender will get his hand in the passing lane. The counter is to send player 2 backdoor. This is keyed by the 4-man reading this, and he must then take a dribble or two toward player 2. This action keys the 5-man to pop up to the top of the key. Player 5 popping to the top is called "Samford." (We picked up this option while watching Samford University game tapes. That's where it got its name.) Once in the Samford set, which is a five-out alignment, player 5 will have two options. The first is to dribble at the wing and send him backdoor. The second is to run a strong-side sweep with the wing, which results in a weak side flare.

No matter whether the team runs a drift option or gets into Samford, the offense can be easily reset.

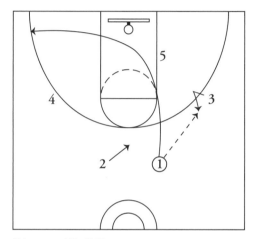

Diagram 17: G-F entry

Diagram 18: F-G pass. Player 3 reads that player 5 isn't open and player 2 can be passed to.

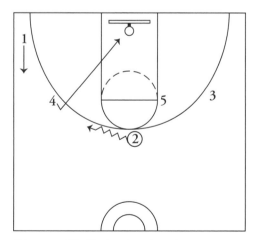

Diagram 19: First cut and post-up opportunity. This is keyed by player 2 sending player 4 backdoor.

Diagram 20: Drift screen. Player 1 passes to player 2 coming off of player 5's drift screen.

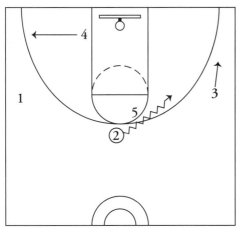
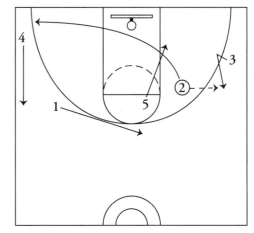

Diagrams 21 and 22: Drift screen. Player 2 isn't open, so he penetrates and resets the offense.

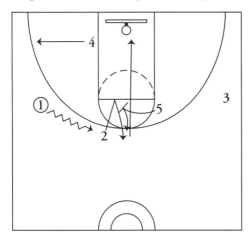
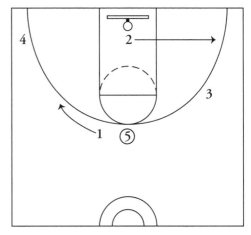

Diagrams 23 and 24: Samford initiation. Player 2 is sent backdoor because X2 got through 5's screen, and player 5 pops to the top.

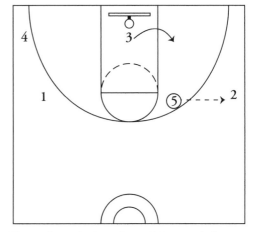

Diagrams 25 and 26: Samford backdoor action. Player 5 reads that player 3 is guarded closely.

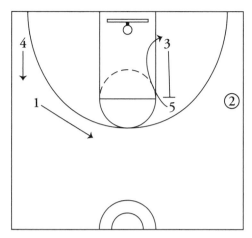
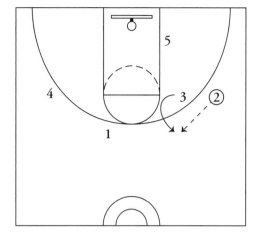

Diagrams 27 and 28: Reset into low post offense from Samford backdoor action

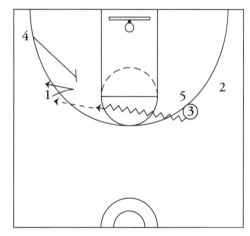

Diagrams 29 and 30: Samford sweep action. Player 3 is guarded loosely.

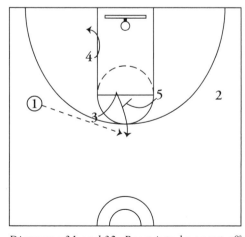
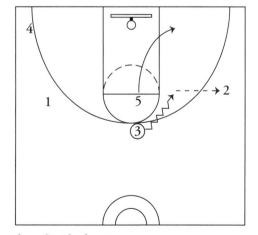

Diagrams 31 and 32: Reset into low post offense from Samford sweep action

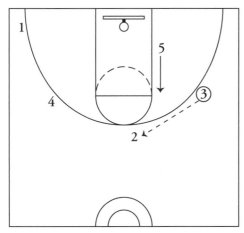 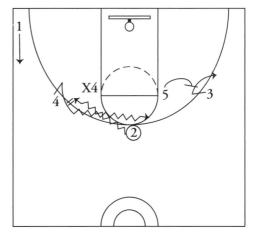

Diagrams 33 and 34: An F-G pass is made, and player 4 sweeps with player 2 rather than cutting backdoor. This would be keyed by player 4 being guarded loosely when player 2 receives the pass from player 3. Instead of running a drift, the team runs a strong-side sweep and weak-side flare option.

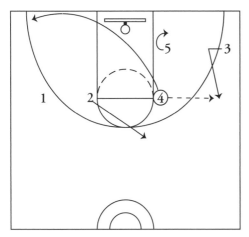 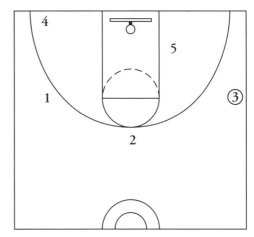

Diagrams 35 and 36: Resetting the offense when a sweep is run, rather than a drift

Pinch-Post Phase

The pinch-post phase is keyed by an F-G pass, which calls for the post to cut to the pinch-post position. What makes this option different than a drift is the 2-man passing the ball to the 5-man at the pinch post.

As soon as the 3-man sees that player 5 is being passed to, he must drop down to the midcorner so that his man cannot execute a quick double team on 5. There are three different options or actions that can be executed while running the pinch-post phase. These options are called "away," "under" and "over."

"Away" is a good first option to teach because it is the simplest of the three options. It is named "away" because the point guard will execute a point screen away action after he passes to the 5-man at the pinch post. The way player 2 passes to the 5-man is important. He must make a step-across bounce pass, and player 5 must shield off his man and be able to meet the pass. As soon as player 5 receives the ball, player 2 will sprint away toward player 4 to set a screen on player 4's defender. More often than not, X4 will be guarding player 4 closely. Therefore player 4 will set up for his cut by cutting above the level of the screen, taking X4 higher.

Once player 4 has set up his man, he will plant his outside foot, take his outside hand and knock down X4's denial arm, extending his inside hand toward the basket and backdoor cutting as hard as he can. Player 4 will look for the ball at least two times during his cut. Player 5 is looking to make a bounce pass to player 4. As soon as player 4 has started his backdoor cut, player 2 will step back toward the ball, looking for a shot. The 1-man will sprint up to fill player 4's vacant spot.

Now, here is a wrinkle in the rules. Instead of cutting back out to the side that he came from, player 4 will move over to the strong-side block and wait for the 3-man to get the ball. Once player 3 has the ball, player 4 will execute a back screen on X5, and player 5 will roll down to the basket looking for a feed from player 3. If player 5 does not receive a pass from player 3, player 4 will pop up to the vacant guard spot, looking for a pass from player 3. The ball can be reversed, and the offense can be reset.

A question I've been asked before by both coaches learning this offense and players is, "What happens if the ball is passed to player 2 on the step back move and he reverses the ball to the 1-man?" In this case, player

4 would not set the back screen on X5, he would set the back screen on X2, and player 2 would cut to the basket. The same type of reversal method will reset the offense.

"Under" is the second option we taught. Player 5 will get the ball at the pinch post, and player 2 will backdoor cut as hard as he can looking for a return pass from player 5. If player 2 doesn't receive the ball from player 5, player 5 will pass to the 3-man. Player 2 will then set a little-on-big back screen on X5. If player 5 doesn't receive a pass, player 2 will pop up, looking for the ball. Since player 2 will have the ball at the top of the floor, and also since the pass that player 2 received was an F-G pass, player 5 will have made a cut to the pinch post. From here, a drift or another pinch-post option can be run.

"Over" was the last option we taught. We usually put this option in a couple of weeks prior to our first tournament game. Player 2 will pass the ball to player 5 at the pinch post and then cut over the top of player 5 to set a speed screen on X3. Player 3 steps toward the screen and then backdoor cuts hard. Player 2 will step back toward the ball after setting his speed screen. If player 5 passes to player 2 stepping back, player 3 will set a little-on-big back screen on X5. Player 3 will pop up after setting his screen, and from this position a drift or another pinch-post option can be run.

Diagrams 37 and 38: G-F entry to a F-G pass. This calls player 5 up to the pinch post.

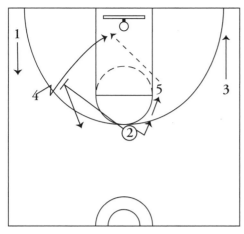 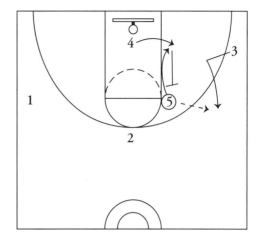

Diagrams 39 and 40: "Away" option. This is keyed by player 2 screening away from player 5.

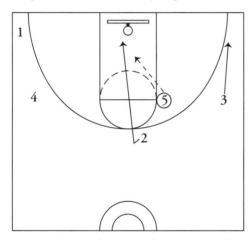 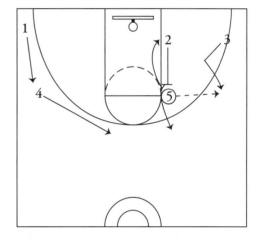

Diagrams 41 and 42: "Under" option. This is keyed by the 2-man cutting backdoor.

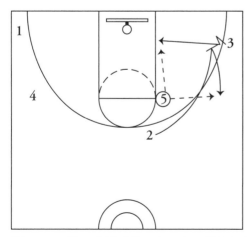 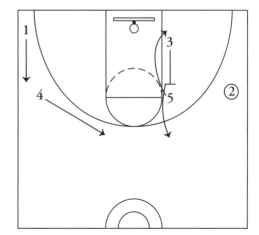

Diagrams 43 and 44: "Over" option. This is keyed by the 2-man cutting over the top of 5.

Pinch-Post Phase Advanced Option

Have player 3 set a screen on player 4.

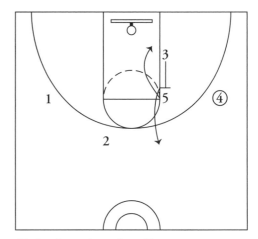

Diagrams 45 and 46: This was just an option we added to keep player 1 on his toes.

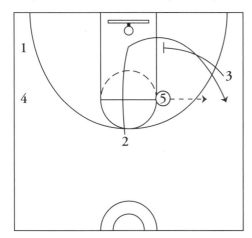

Diagrams 47 and 48: We found at the time that this made the pass to the wing easier to achieve.

Forward Dribble

This phase is executed when the 3-man (right strong-side forward) catches the ball and reads two things quickly. First, the post is unable to receive a pass. Second, the 2-man (or guard at the top of the key) is being guarded closely, so passing to him isn't an option. The strong-side forward must set this phase into action by dribbling hard to the stong-side read spot. From here, there will be two quick backdoor opportunities, a ball reversal opportunity and a high post opportunity.

Player 3 will drive hard to the read spot, looking to pass off of the dribble to player 2, who will be cutting hard to the basket. As soon as player 5 sees player 3 execute the forward dribble, he must step out to the short corner and keep his defender occupied. If player 2 doesn't receive the pass, he will cut out to the strong-side corner.

Player 4 will watch player 2 in front of him. As soon as he recognizes the forward dribble phase and player 2 cuts, player 4 will step into his read spot. More often than not, X4 will be guarding him closely, so player 4 will wait to see 3's pump fake at him (player 3 will have picked up his dribble) and then cut backdoor. The key to player 4's timing is that he must wait until player 2 is out of the way and player 3 makes his pass fake. If player 4 doesn't receive a pass, he will cut back out to the same side of the floor. If player 4 isn't played closely, he will make a high cut and fill the vacant guard spot for ball reversal.

Player 1 will watch player 4 in front of him. As soon as he sees player 4 step into his read spot, he will sprint up to player 4's vacant original spot. Player 1 will wait to see what player 4 does. If player 4 cuts backdoor, player 1 must L-cut up to the vacant guard spot. If player 4 makes a high cut for ball reversal, player 1 will remain in his current position.

Ball reversal equals a screen down for the post. Player 3 will move down to the mid post and set a down screen on X5, and player 5 will cut to the vacant guard spot. It is important that player 3 stays high—you don't want him to drop down to the low post. Once player 5 has received the ball from player 4 (who will have made a high cut), player 5 has two options.

The first high post option is a direct pass to player 2. If the direct pass isn't there, player 5 will sweep with player 2.

The second high post option is a sweep look. On the sweep the player receiving the sweep from player 5 will run off player 5's sweep and player 3's ball screen. The player with the ball is looking for a shot off the screens or a pass to the players executing the weak-side flare option.

I was often asked how a team could run a forward dribble with a post player that was not perimeter friendly. The answer came from watching tapes from a high school team that ran the Princeton offense. Instead of screening down for the post, you have the post set a flare screen. Resetting the offense is then simple. See "forward dribble for a nonperimeter post" in the diagrams.

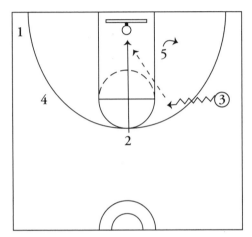 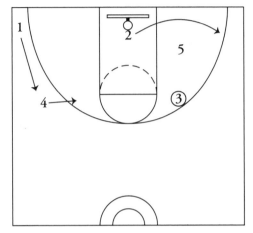

Diagrams 49 and 50: The 3-man drives to the read spot, sending player 2 backdoor.

 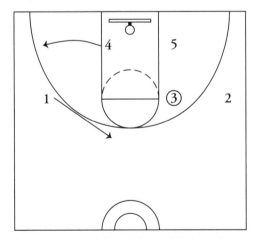

Diagrams 51 and 52: The 4-man is guarded closely and cuts backdoor. Player 1 fills to the guard spot.

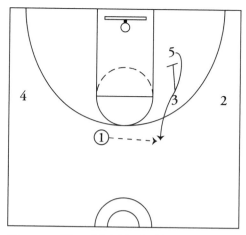
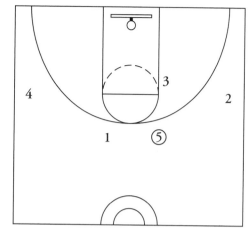

Diagrams 53 and 54: The ball is reversed to player 1, therefore player 3 will pick down for player 5.

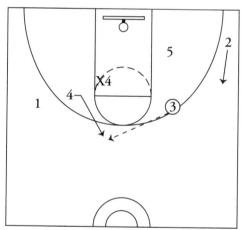
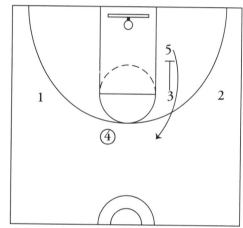

Diagrams 55 and 56: Player 4 is guarded loosely, so he makes a high cut.

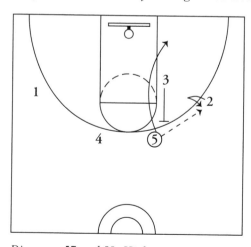
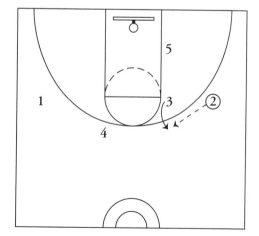

Diagrams 57 and 58: High post option one: direct pass to player 2 and backscreen.

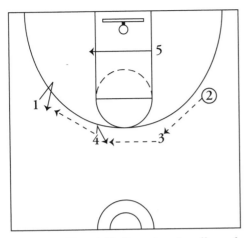 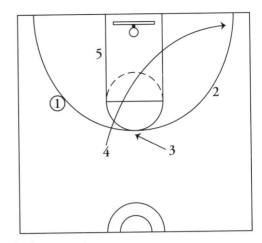

Diagrams 59 and 60: Resetting the offense from high post option one

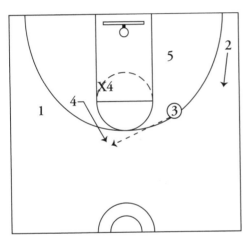 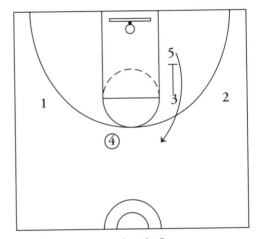

Diagrams 61 and 62: High post option two: strong-side sweep to weak-side flare

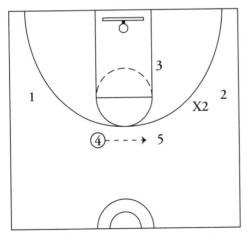 

Diagram 63: Player 5 cannot pass to player 2= sweep.

Diagram 64: 3 sets a ball screen on X2. 1 and 4 position for the w-s flare action.

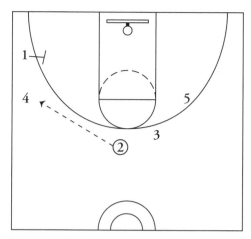

Diagram 65: 2 passes to 4.

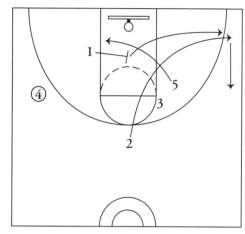

Diagram 66: 1 screens for 5 and exits out to w-s corner. 2 cuts through.

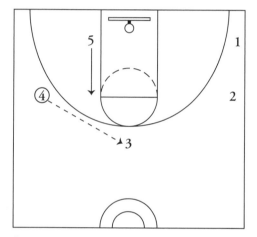

Diagram 67: 3 goes to the top to low post.

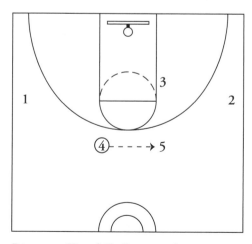

Diagrams 68 and 69: Strong-side sweep = w-s flare

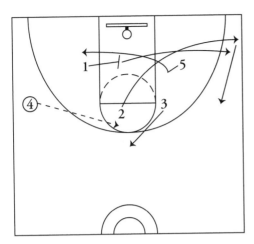 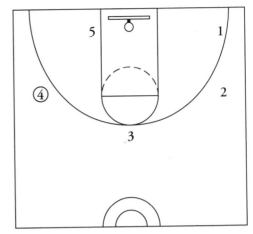

Diagrams 70 and 71: Resetting the offense from high post option two. 2 cuts through to the weak-side wing, 3 bumps up to the top of floor, and 1 screens for 5 and cuts to the weak-side corner.

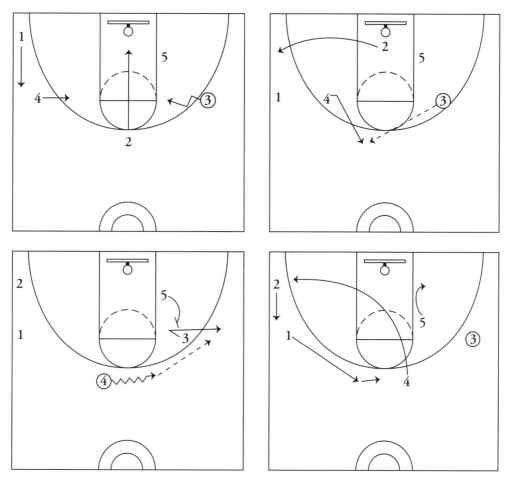

Diagrams 72, 73, 74 and 75: Forward dribble for a nonperimeter post. Note: The rule for 2's cut is different here. Instead of cutting to the strong-side corner, he cuts to the weak-side corner.

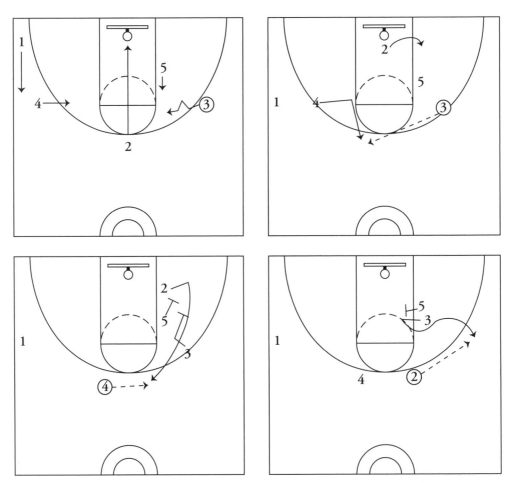

Diagrams 76, 77, 78 and 79: The New Jersey Nets option for keeping the post low

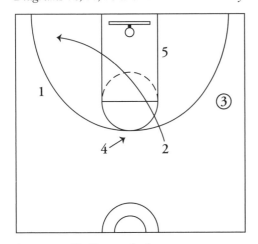

Diagrams 80: Now in the lost post set

Chapter 5
The High Spread Offense

This offense is a great way to spread the court and run the clock. It also offers several scoring opportunities that are based on the same rules of the low post offense. In fact, many teams that run the Princeton offense even use it as a default offense when the low post offense breaks down. Princeton, Air Force and Northwestern call this offense "chin." This name stems from the fact that the offense's cadence is the point guard pointing at his chin. There are many different ways to enter into this offense, but circle and forwards out are probably the most popular.

G-G-F Entry

As the ball is being reversed, Player 5 will wait until Player 4 catches the ball. Once Player 4 has the ball, Player 5 will set a back screen on X1 as high as possible. Player 1 will cut, looking for the ball. Player 5 has to make a read as to what his next move will be. He will either set a drift screen for Player 2 or duck in toward the pinch post, looking for the ball. Remember this timing: Players 1 and 5 wait until Player 4 has the ball before they screen and cut.

Diagram 81

Diagram 82

Drift Option

If player X2 jumps to the ball (after player 2 has passed to Player 4), then player 5 will set a drift screen on X2. Player 2 will set his man up for the screen and come off of it, looking for a shot or driving opportunity. Player 1 will exit out to the strong-side corner.

Diagram 83

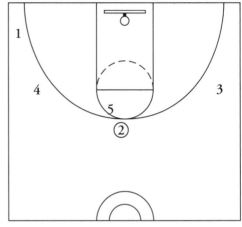

Diagram 84

Resetting the Offense from a Drift

If player 2 does not shoot, he will dribble over to the vacant guard spot and look to pass to player 3. This action pulls player 4 up to the other vacant guard spot and player 1 up to the vacant forward spot. Player 5 will stay at his current pinch post position; he doesn't follow the ball. He gets ready to set a back screen on player X4 when player 3 catches the ball.

Diagram 85

Diagram 86

What Happens if Player 2 Isn't Open Off of the Drift Screen?

In this scenario, player 4 must follow this rule: He must dribble at player 2 and send him backdoor. If player 2 doesn't receive a pass, he will exit out to the open corner, and player 5 will pop up for ball reversal. From here, the team runs Samford.

Diagram 87

Diagram 88

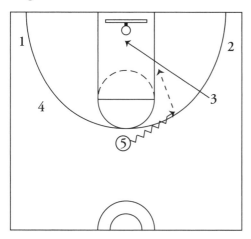

Diagram 89: Player 5 sends 3 backdoor, or...

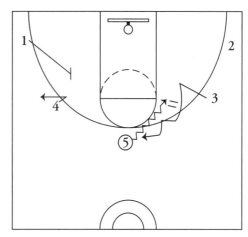

Diagram 90: Player 5 and 3 run a sweep.

Player 5 Ducks into the Pinch Post Rather than Setting a Drift

If Player 5 sees that X2 stayed and denied Player 2 the ball rather than jumping toward the ball, Player 5 will dive into the vacant pinch post, looking for the ball. Player 5 has several options upon catching the ball at the pinch post: He can shoot, drive, reverse his pivot and kick to the opposite side, or dribble at one of the players on the weak side to send them backdoor or sweep with them.

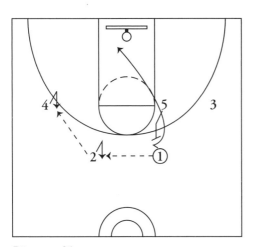

Diagram 91

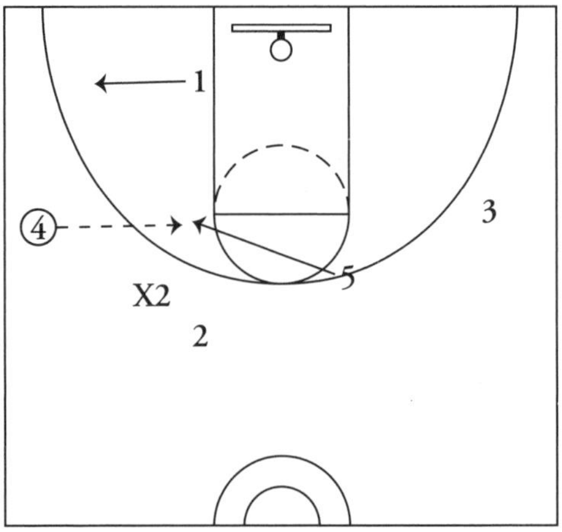

Diagram 92

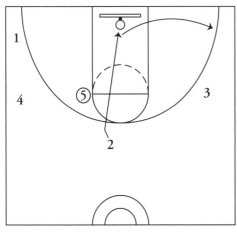

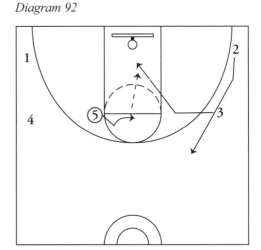

Diagram 93: Player 5 sends 2 backdoor, or...

Diagram 94: Player 5 dribbles at player 3 and sends him backdoor. 2 must sprint to the vacant G. position.

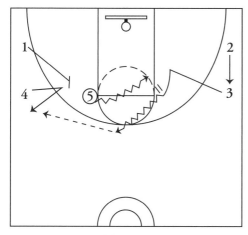

Diagram 95: Dribble across sweep action

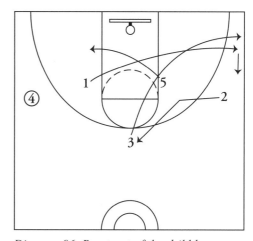

Diagram 96: Reset out of the dribble across sweep action

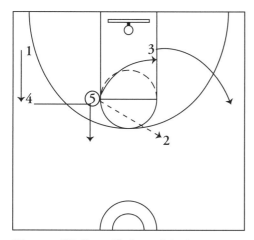

Diagram 97: Reset if player 3 isn't open on his backcourt

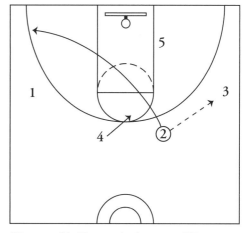

Diagram 98: Now in the low-post GF entry

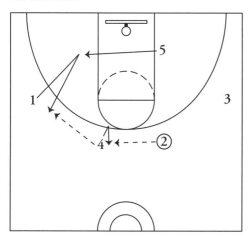

Diagram 99: Swing entry

One of the Players in a Guard Spot Passes the Ball Directly to Player 5

This pass keys the "clone" set. Clone can be found in the set play section. For the sake of simplicity, I have diagrammed clone here and added how to get the high spread offense reset if clone doesn't produce a shot.

Diagram 100

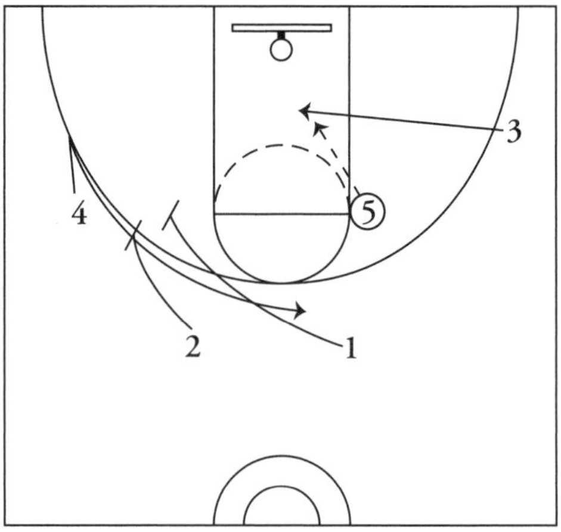

Diagram 101

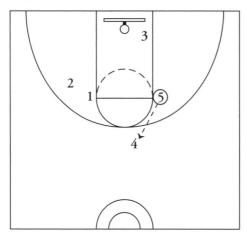

Diagram 102: Player 5 passes to player 4 cutting off the double score.

Diagram 103: Player 5 passes to 4, who passes to 1, cutting off 2's flare pick. The timing is 2 and 1 work together when 4 gets the ball.

Resetting the Offense if Clone Doesn't Provide a Shot

The 5-man will set a drift screen on the passer located at the top of the key. A drift can be run, a backdoor cut can be executed, and/or Samford can be run. It all depends on what the defense does and what the player with the ball reads.

Diagram 104

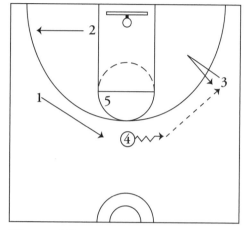

Diagram 105

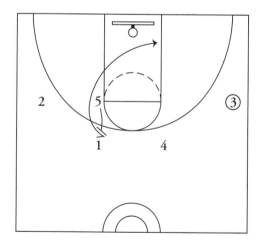

Diagram 106

The Ball Goes G-F when the Post is Located on the Strong Side

This pass will key a back screen, or "UCLA action." Player 5 will set a back screen on player X1 as high as he can. Player 5 will pop up to the vacant guard spot after screening. Players 2 and 4 will watch player 5 and if he gets the ball, they must float down a spot. Once player 5 has the ball, we are now in Samford.

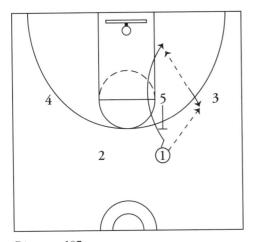

Diagram 107

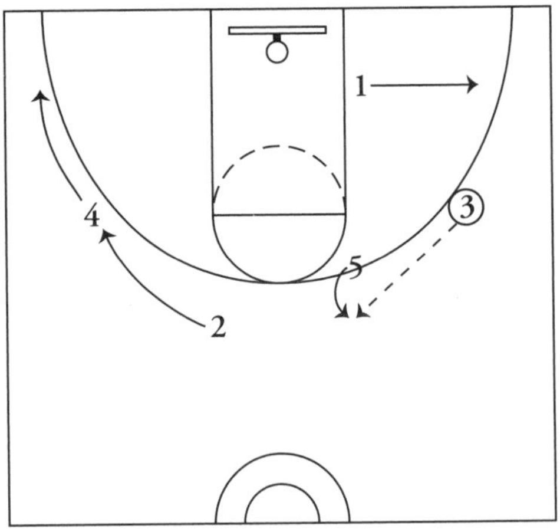

Diagram 108

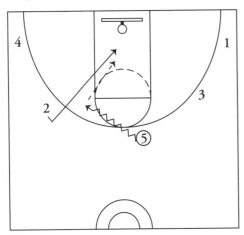

Diagram 109: Samford backdoor option

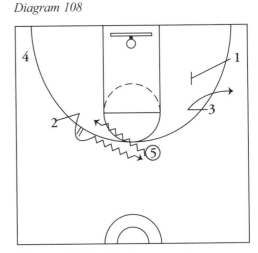

Diagram 110:Samford sweep option

Some teams run the same high post option that was run with the forward dribble pass:

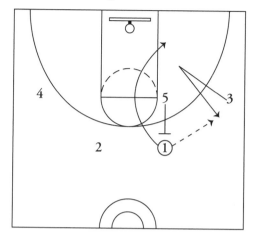

Diagram 111: 1 to 3

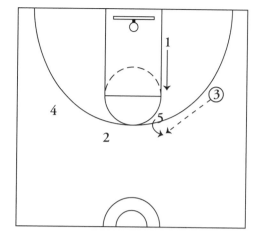

Diagram 112: 3 back to 5

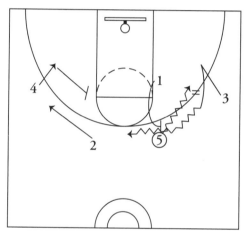

Diagram 113: Sweep

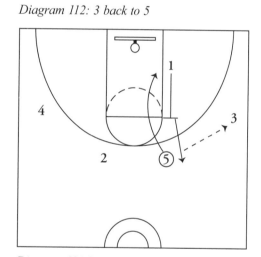

Diagram 114:Direct pass to 3 = back screen

What if I Don't Want my 5-Man Handling the Ball up Top?

Some teams run a zipper or screen-down action so that the post player doesn't have to handle the ball a lot. The ball gets reversed around the perimeter, then players 2 and 5 set a staggered screen down for the 1-man. Player 2 fills the vacant guard spot, and player 5 steps into his spot at the pinch post. Now the offense is reset.

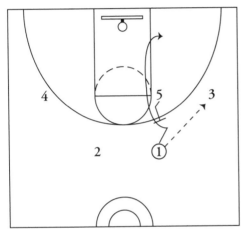

Diagram 115

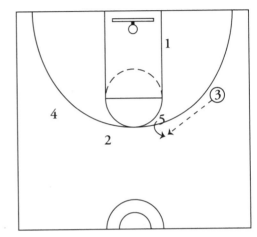

Diagram 116

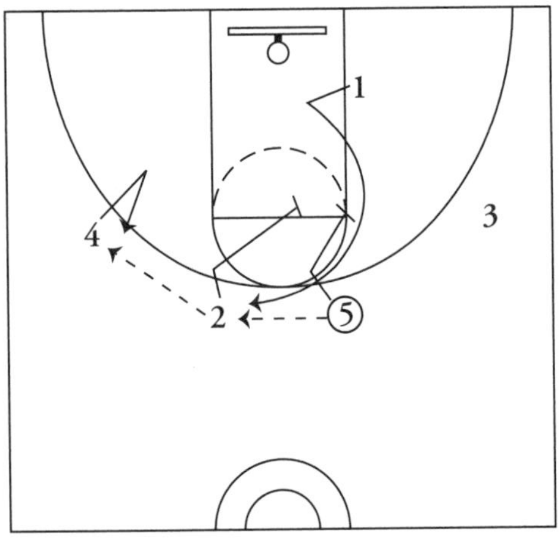

Diagram 117

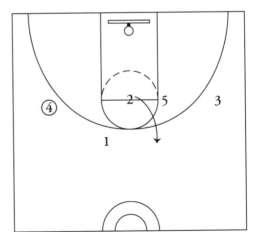

Diagram 118

Chapter 6
Advanced Entries into the Low Post and High Spread Offense

The advanced entries in this chapter can be adapted to the skill level of your team. For example, my own teams would not use all of these entries during one season. As skill and talent levels changed from season to season, we would use different entries that were best suited for our teams. A lot of these entries would be used to shorten the game against teams that were far more athletic than ours.

Circle

This is used to break pressure and open up to the forwards. Against teams that pressured us hard, we could use this to get a couple of lay-up opportunities. The players starting out in the guard spots look to backdoor. Players starting in the forward spots look to slip their screens to counter switching or when their defenders jumped above the level of the screen to help. If the player can't get the ball to the forward, then he should run it again.

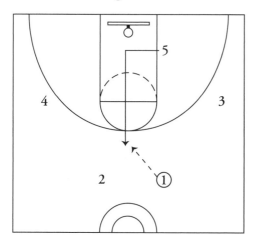 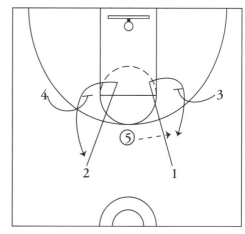

Diagram 119 and 120: Timing – As soon as player 5 sees circle has been called, he sprints up to the top.

Getting into the Low Post Offense After Running Circle

The forwards are always looking to step back into their spots after screening (unless they can slip the screen). Once the strong-side forward has the ball, you're in business. The passer simply cuts through (guard-forward pass). The 2-man cuts to the top of the key.

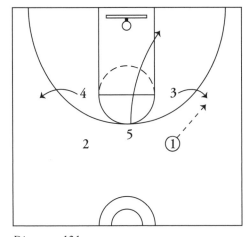
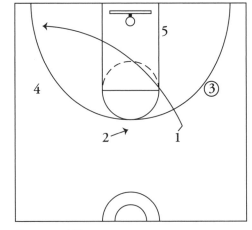

Diagram 121   *Diagram 122*

X

This is run if one of the guards executed a backdoor cut when running circle. This is a read that the players make. It's simple: If one of the guards back cuts, then we are in X. This entry can be called out by the coach or point guard. We run this entry against teams that overplayed the passing lanes.

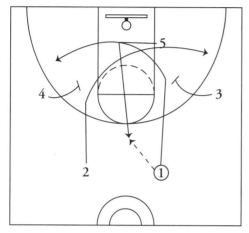 

Diagram 123   *Diagram 124: Now in low post offense*

Sweep

We ran this entry against teams that played great helpside and pressure defense.

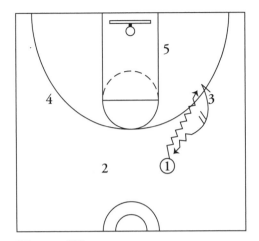

Diagram 125

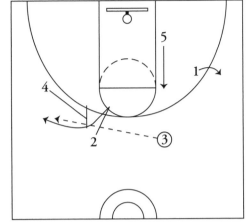

Diagram 126: Now in low post offense

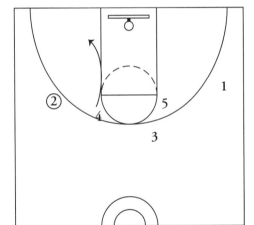

Diagram 127

Diagram 128: Now in low post offense.

Getting into the Low Post Offense from a Sweep Entry

We did this two different ways. The first year we used the Princeton offense, we just got back into low post by having the 4-man cut through. Everyone else bumped up a spot except for player 5, who dove to the strong-side block. The next year, we went right into a drift. The following diagrams show the year-one method of getting into the low post offense from a sweep entry.

Diagram 129

Diagram 130: 4 screens for 5 and exits out opposite. 3 cuts through and 1 fills up the top.

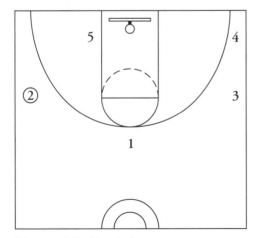

Diagram 131: Now in low post

Using a Drift to Get Back into the Low Post Offense from the Sweep Entry

Instead of having player 4 cut through, have him slide down to the low block and post up. Players 5 and 3 will then execute a drift up top. This would get us back into the low post offense.

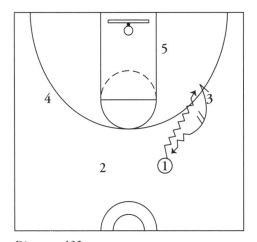

Diagram 132

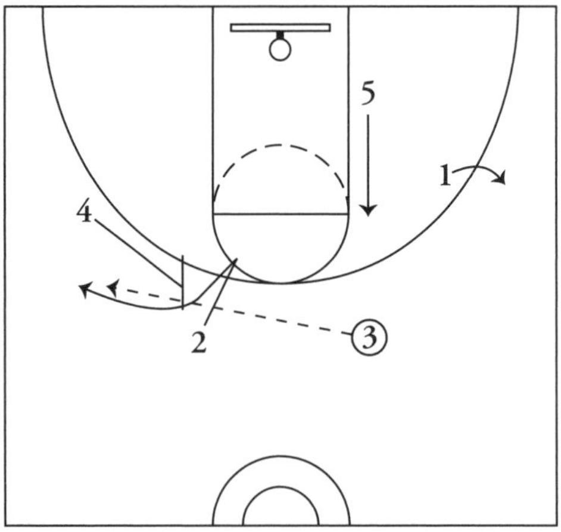

Diagram 133: *Now in low post offense*

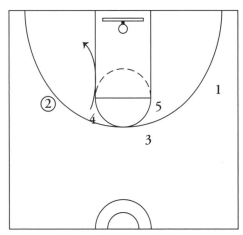

Diagram 134

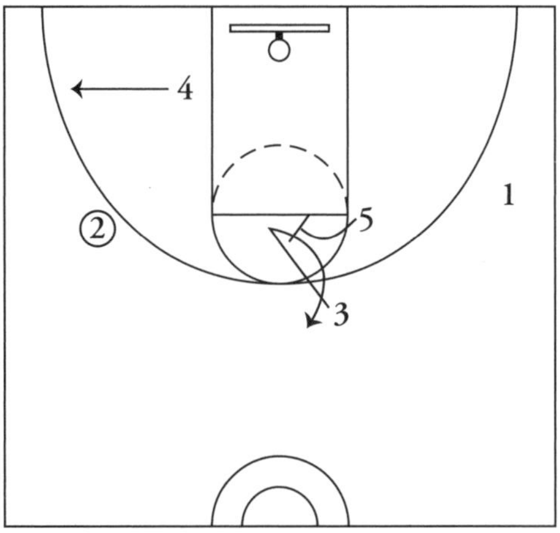

Diagram 135: *Now in low post offense*

Weakside

We would run this against teams that employed a run-and-jump defense at the half-court level. We also ran this against athletic teams that pressured the lanes and the ball.

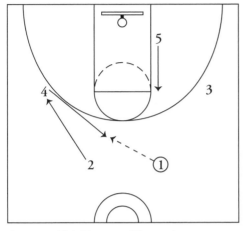

Diagram 136: Timing – Player 4 cuts as soon as player 1 crosses the half-court line.

Diagram 137: Player 4 dribbles at player 2 to send him backdoor.

Diagram 138: Player 4 picks his dribble up = sweep.

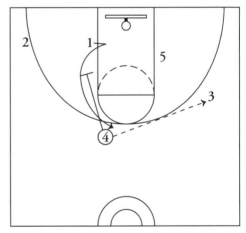

Diagram 139: Player 4 reverses = screen down for 1-man.

Loop

This is an L-cut entry to open guard-guard reversal. The timing here is very important. Player 4 doesn't make his L-cut until player 2 has crossed the free-throw line. Player 4 catches and looks to reverse to player 2. Player 5 waits until player 2 catches on the wing to make his block to block cut.

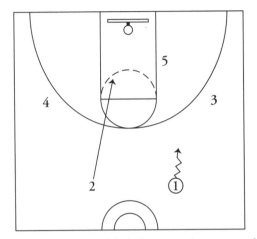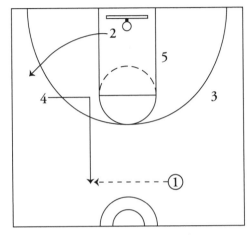

Diagrams 140 and 141: Timing – As soon as player 2 crosses the free-throw line, player 4 executes his L-cut.

Push

We would run this play to open up the 5-man and to relieve wing pressure. As soon as player 3 sees player 1 wave at him, he cuts down and sets a screen for player 5. Player 2 has to make an exaggerated V-cut here because more often than not, player 1 will pick up his dribble. We did have one guard that was good enough to use a roll dribble to initiate a forward dribble or to use a "roll out" move if player 5 wasn't open.

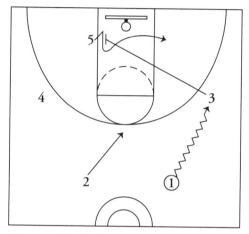

Diagram 142: Little-on-big screen (players 3 and 5)

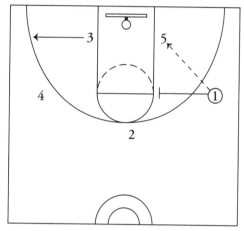

Diagram 143: Now in low post offense

Pull

We would run this to get a hot point guard open off a drift early in the offense. It is important to note that this has to be a called entry. If player 1 would wave at player 2, he would assume that we were running a wave option. Player 4 must open up to the ball immediately after setting the back screen on player 2. Players 5 and 1 run a drift up top when player 4 catches the ball.

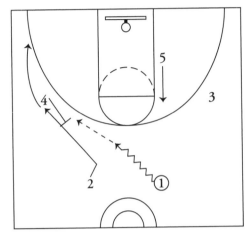

Diagram 144

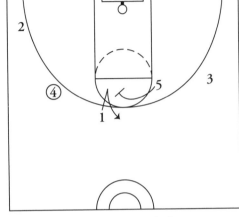

Diagram 145: Right into a drift

Samford as an Entry

We ran this when we had a 6'1" post who could handle the ball. We also ran this against teams that had very athletic guards but slower posts. We would have our post player bring up the ball.

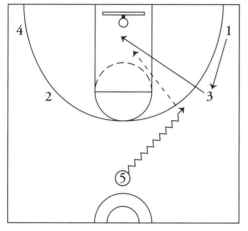

Diagram 146

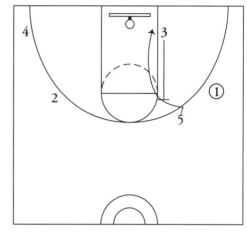

Diagram 147: Little-on-big screening action

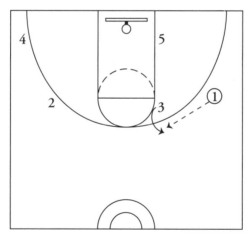

Diagram 148: Now in low post offense

Samford vs. Flat Triangle Defense

If X1 was gapping or playing in a flat triangle position in the passing lane, 5 would read this and dribble at X1. This action tells 1 that 5 is calling for a sweep. Strong-side sweep = weak-side flare.

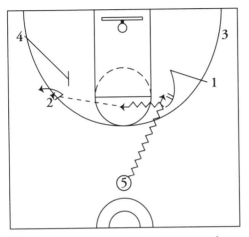

Diagram 149: Strong-side sweep = weak-side flare.

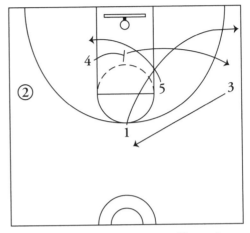

Diagram 150: Now in low post offense. 4 screens for 5, 1 and 3 cut and bump up.

Forwards Out

Run this play to kill the clock or to force an aggressive defense to chase the offensive players. This is a great entry if you have the lead. This entry will put the defense to sleep and afford the offense backdoor opportunities. It can be run over and over again.

Diagram 151: Strong-side sweep = weak-side flare.

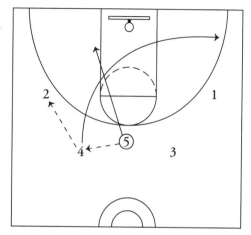

Diagram 152: Now in low post offense

Wave

This is a one guard front entry. It eliminates having to get the ball to the wing to initiate the offense. This also gets the post above the free-throw line early and frees up the lane. Any of the three pinch post options can be run during a wave entry. We called it a wave because the point guard waves his hand at the 2-guard in order to get him to cut through. The 2-man sets a screen on the 5-man prior to exiting out to the corner. Player 1 must make a left-handed bounce pass to player 5.

Away

The first set that we taught was the "away" set. This is the easiest to learn.

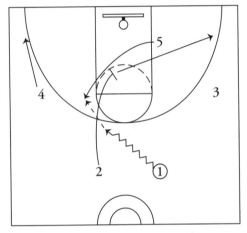

Diagram 153: Player 2 screens and exits to the opposite corner.

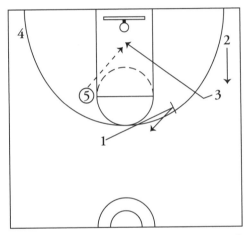

Diagram 154: Player 1 screens away toward player 3, who cuts backdoor. Player 2 sprints up.

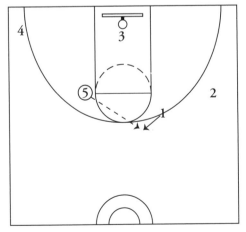

Diagram 155: Player 5 passes to player 1 for a shot or to drive.

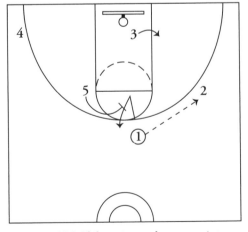

Diagram 156: If there is no shot, reset into low post.

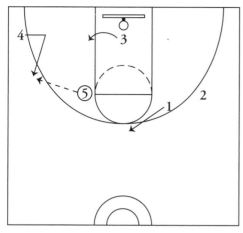

Diagram 157: If player 5 passes to player 4, go to back screen action.

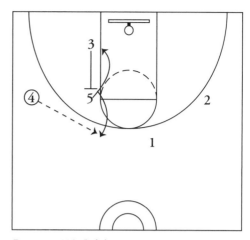

Diagram 158:]If there is no shot, reset into low post.

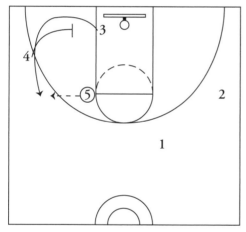

Diagram 159: Player 4 can also screen for player 3 (5 to 3).

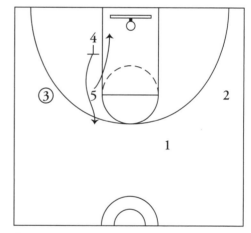

Diagram 160: Now in the low post

Over

We ran "Over" against teams that pressured the passing lanes. The first backdoor option will produce results.

Diagram 161: Player 2 picks for player 5, and player 4 drops. Player 1 to player 5.

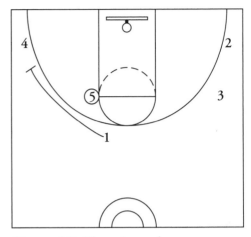

Diagram 162: Player 1 speed screens over player 5 toward player 4.

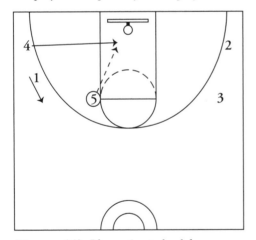

Diagram 163: Player 4 cuts backdoor.

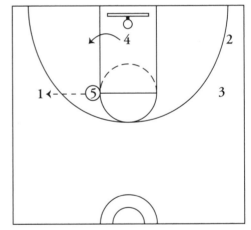

Diagram 164: Player 5 passes to player 1 for shot.

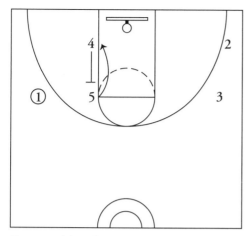

Diagram 165: Player 4 cuts backdoor.

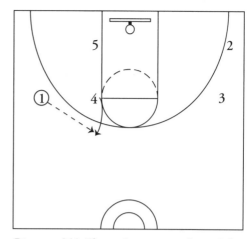

Diagram 166: Player 5 passes to player 1 for shot.

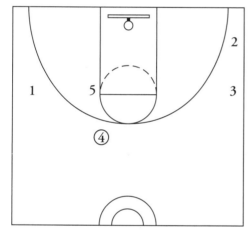

Diagram 167: 4 can pass to 5 for pinch post action or dribble toward 3 for a drift.

Under

We ran "Under" against teams that pressured the ball very hard.

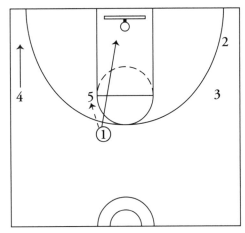

Diagram 168: Player 1 passes to player 5 and backdoor cuts.

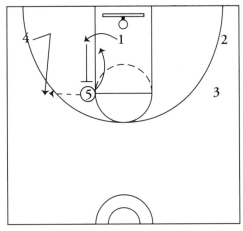

Diagram 169: Player 5 to player 4 = backscreen action.

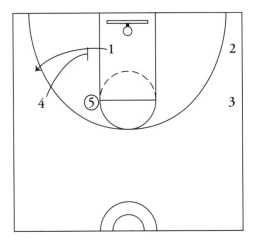

Diagrams 170-172: 4 can also set a screen on X1. This provides another look to the set.

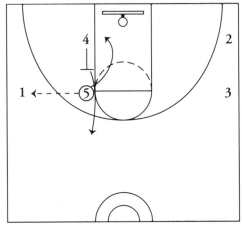

Diagram 171.

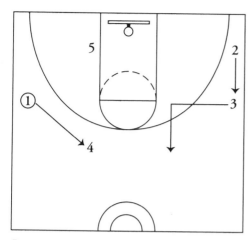

Diagram 172. Resetting the offense, option 1.
Player 3 fills the vacant G position.

Resetting the offense, option 2. Have 4 run a drift with player 3 or pass to 5 for a pinch post spot.

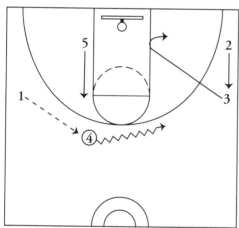

Diagram 173: Drift

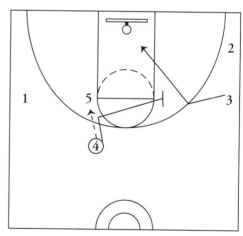

Diagram 174: Pinch post offense

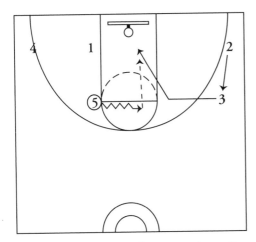 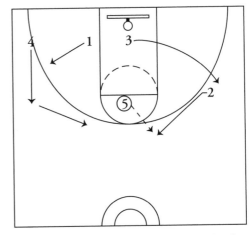

Diagram 175: Advanced option—player 5 takes a dribble at player 3 to send him backdoor. Player 2 sprints up.

Diagram 176: If there is no shot, reset back into the low-post offense.

What if Player 5 is Unable to Accept a Pass After the Wave has been Initiated?

In this case, the point guard must execute a roll out. Here, he executes a roll dribble to change directions and sends the 3-man backdoor. Player 2 is sprinting up to the wing to receive a pass from player 1. We now go directly into a drift with players 5 and 1.

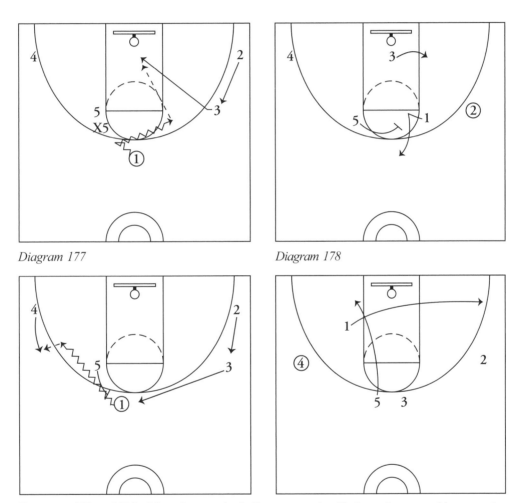

Diagram 177

Diagram 178

Diagrams 179 and 180: May also use the ball screen option if player 5 was unable to receive the initial pass from player 1.

Chapter 7
Special Situation Plays

Although we did not run a lot of other sets or quick hitters, we did use a couple for end-of-quarter or game situations. We didn't run all of these in a single season; we usually had three. We always wanted our specials to be run out of the same offensive alignment as the low post offense. We really made an effort to save our specials for the second halves of games. We also felt it was important that all of our specials ended up in the same alignment as low post so that they could flow together. It is also important to note that we used our sets most often if we were trailing late in the game.

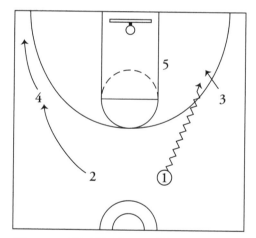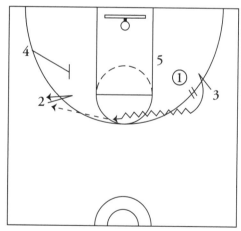

Diagrams 181-182: Timing: Player 4 must wait until player 3 comes off of player 5's screen to set his flare screen for player 2. Player 2 doesn't move until player 4 does.

One Guard

Run this play to get a quick three-point opportunity or post feed.

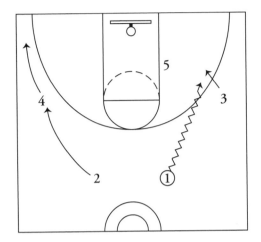

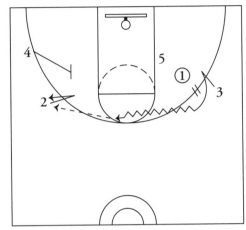

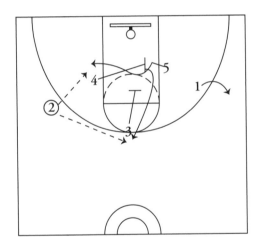

Diagram 183-185: Timing: Player 4 must wait until player 3 comes off of player 5's screen to set his flare screen for player 2. Player 2 doesn't move until player 4 does.

Wisconsin

Run this for a quick three-point opportunity.

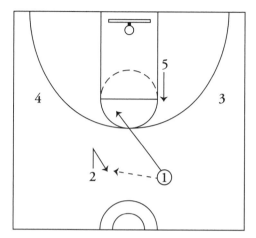

Diagram 186: Player 1 to player 2.

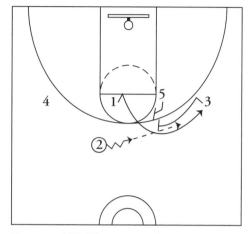

Diagram 187: Players 5 and 3 set a double flare.

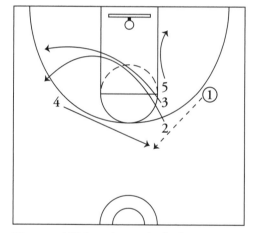

Diagram 188:1 to 4, now in the low post, ready to run a drift or fixed-post option.

Purple

Run this for a quick three-point opportunity.

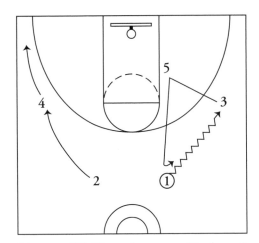

Diagram 189: Player 1 sweeps with player 3.

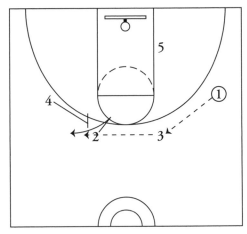

Diagram 190: When player 3 catches, flare.

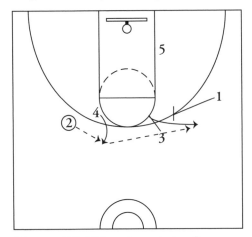

Diagram 191: If there is no shot, reflare.

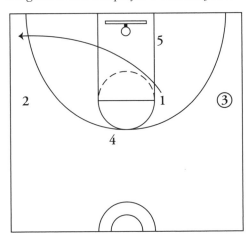

Diagram 192: Now in the low post offense.

Miami

Run this play for a quick three or backdoor.

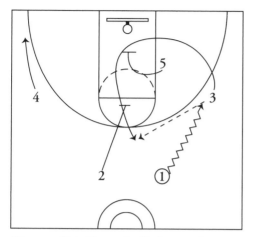

Diagram 194: Player 3 off of two picks.

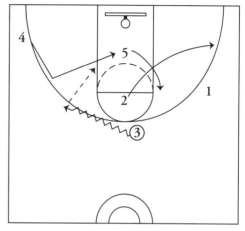

Diagram 195: Player 3 for player 4 on backdoor cut.

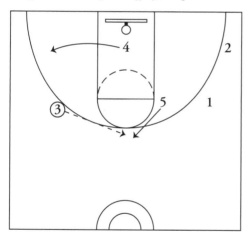

Diagram 196: If there is no shot, go to Samford play.

Invert

Run this play for a quick backdoor or high to low post feed.

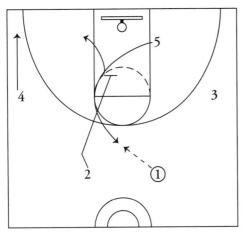

Diagram 197: Player 2 sets a pick for player 5. Player 1 passes to player 5.

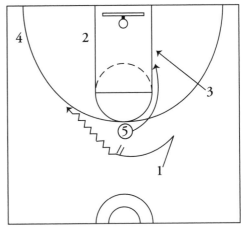

Diagram 198: Player 5 back to player 1, player 3 drops.

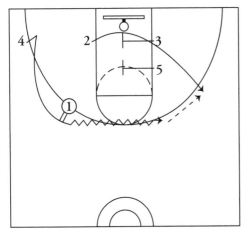

Diagram 199: Players 1 and 4 sweep, player 2 comes off the double screen.

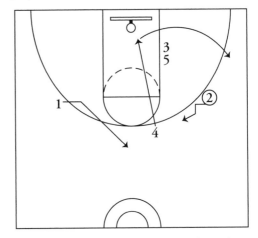

Diagram 200: Player 2 passes to player 1. Player 5 picks for player 3.

Diagram 201: Player 2 passes to player 1. Player 5 picks for player 3.

Diagram 202: High low and double pick action

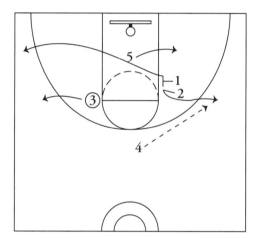

Diagram 203: Now in low post offense

Double

Run this play for a quick lay-up opportunity.

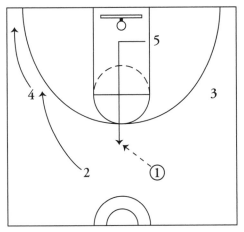

Diagram 204: Player 1 passes to player 5, players 2 and 4 drop.

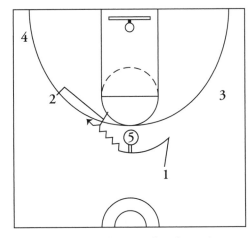

Diagram 205: Ball screen for player 1

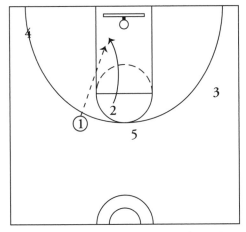

Diagram 206: Player 1 passes to player 5, players 2 and 4 drop.

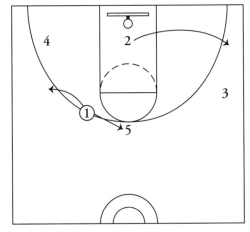

Diagram 207: Now in low post offense

Green Bay

Run this play for a quick lay-up or post-feed opportunity.

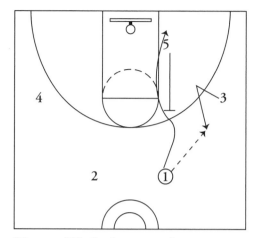

Diagram 208: Backscreen action

Diagram 209: Double for player 1

Diagram 210: Double for player 5 and screen the screener action

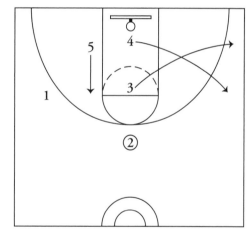

Diagram 211: Now in low post offense

Clone

Run this play for a backdoor or three-point opportunity.

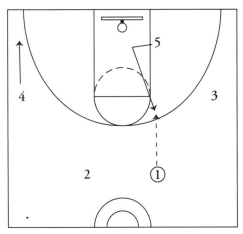

Diagram 212: Player 1 passes to player 5, player 4 drops.

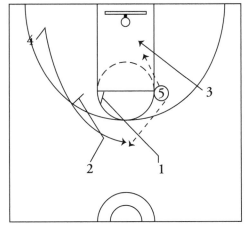

Diagram 213: Backdoor and double action

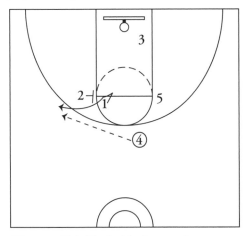

Diagram 214: Weak-side flare action

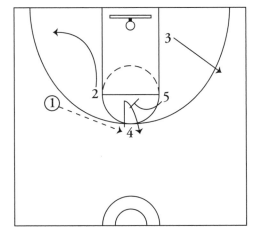

Diagram 215: If there is no shot, go into the drift phase.

South

Run this for a quick three or backdoor.

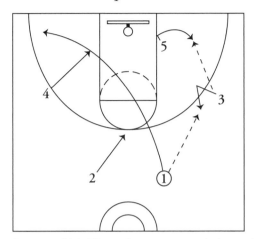

Diagram 216: Player 5 steps out, and player 4 drops.

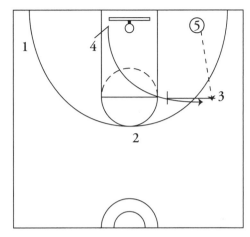

Diagram 217: Player 3 picks for player 4. Player 5 passes to player 4.

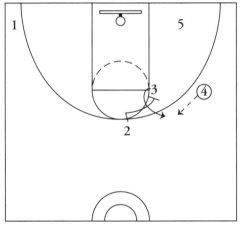

Diagram 218: Pick the picker action

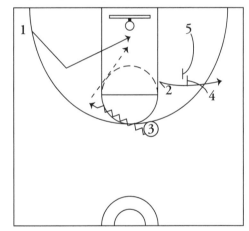

Diagram 219: Backdoor or double flare action

Laker

Run this play for a high to low pass or for a driving opportunity for a mismatched forward.

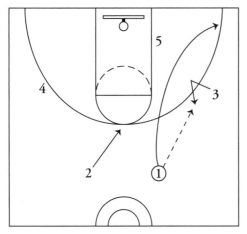

Diagram 220: Player 1 strong-side cuts.

Diagram 221: Player 2 catches = player 4 to pinch.

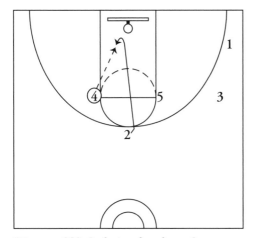

Diagram 222: Isolation for player 2

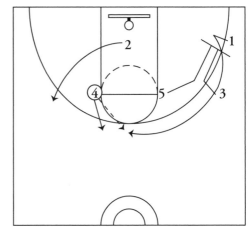

Diagram 223: Double screen for player 1

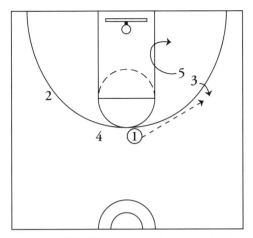

Diagram 224: If there is no shot, pass back to player 3.

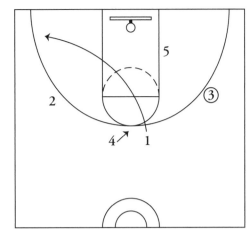

Diagram 225: Now in the low post

Chapter 8
Review of the Basics

The following is a simple review of the basics of the Princeton offense. This will help you begin to teach the offense and plan your practices.

  I. Guard-forward pass = The passer cuts through to weak-side corner. The forward's first look is to the post.

 II. Post feed = Elbow screen or forward drop phase.

    A. Straight cut.

    B. Backdoor.

    C. Slip.

    D. Forward drop.

III. Forward-guard pass = drift or pinch post phases.

IV. Forward cannot pass the ball to the post player or the player at the top of the key = forward dribble phase.

A General Overview of Practice Weeks 1 and 2 During the First Year

  I. Used the whole-part-whole teaching method. Show it to the players, break it down into drills, bring them back and show them the whole again

 II. Make every drill directly correlate to the offense

    A. Shooting drills

    B. Ball handling drills

    C. Rebounding and transition drills

    D. Read/breakdown drills

III. Teach the guard the forward entry skill first

    A. 5-on-0 full court to 3-on-3 side-court breakdowns

  B. 5-on-5 full court vs. soft and hard defense. Get the strong-side wing man open

 IV. The second skill to teach is the guard-to-guard entry

  A. 5-on-0 full court to 3-on-3 side-court breakdowns

  B. 5-on-5 full court vs. soft and hard defense. Players 1 and 2 must work together to get the ball reversed

 V. The first phase to teach is the elbow screen phase

  A. Feed the post properly to 2-on-2 breakdowns

  B. Straight cut read to 3-on-3 breakdowns

  C. Backdoor cut read to 3-on-3 breakdowns

  D. Screener slip vs. the switch to 3-on-3 breakdowns

  E. 5-on-0 review of all options

  F. 5-on-5 with defense allowing the ball to be fed to post

   1. The coach tells the defense how to play (discreetly) hard or soft on cutter to force the cutters to make proper reads

  G. 5-on-5 with good post defense. Make offense feed the post properly using G-F and G-G entries

  H. Start each practice session with a review of previously taught phase and options, then back to yesterday's breakdowns

 VI. The second phase to teach is the drift phase (F-G pass)

  A. Explain that the forward-guard pass action starts this phase

  B. Explain that this phase is run because player 3 can pass to player 2

  C. Teach the post how to cut to the pinch post

  D. Divide the guards and posts up and go 2-on-2 with the guards and 1-on 1-with the posts (with a coach passing) to emphasize the coaching points

  E. 5-on-0 to 4-on-4 breakdowns

   1. G-F pass vs. soft defense

   2. Post-cut timing

   3. First cut and post-up option

F. Drift screen & cut

G. 5-on-0 review of what was just taught

H. 5-on-0 drift phase to reset of the offense

I. 5-on-5 G-F entry into drift option vs. soft defense

J. 5-on-5 G-G entry into drift option vs. soft defense

K. 5-on-5 using both entries and phases

VII. The third phase to teach is the pinch post phase

A. Explain that the forward-guard action starts this phase

B. Explain why this phase is run

C. 5-on-0 pinch post "Away" option

D. Break guards and posts up into separate groups

1. Guards are taught how to pass to the post

2. Posts review how to cut to pinch post and what to look for

E. 5-on-0 review of "Away" option to 4-on-4 breakdowns

F. 5-on-5 G-F entry into pinch post "Away" option

G. 5-on-5 G-G entry into pinch post "Away" option

H. 5-on-5 using both entries into any option

VIII. The fourth phase to teach is the forward dribble phase

A. 5-on-0 first cut

B. 3-on-3 breakdowns passing to the first cutter

C. 5-on-0 second cut

D. 3-on-3 breakdowns passing to the second cutter

E. 5-on-0 timing and positioning of the third cutter

F. 5-on-0 screening down for the post to backscreen option

G. 3-on-3 breakdowns of the previous action

H. 5-on-0 review

I. 5-on-5 both entries to forward dribble phase

J. 5-on-5 both entries into any phase

My staff and I created an instructional tape and booklet that helped us teach this offense to our lower-level coaches. Being able to watch how the offense works and how to teach it really helped us.

Princeton-Style Zone Offense vs. Even Front Zones

As player 1 dribbles away from player 5, he wants to pull his defender over to the other side. Player 5 is drifting out to the short corner in an attempt to get behind the weak-side defensive wing. As soon as player 1 gets near the opposite guard spot, player 4 will cut out to the vacant guard spot. He is looking for a pass from player 1. As the ball is in the air, player 5 will set a screen on the strong-side wing defender. Player 3 will drop to the corner. Player 4's first look is to player 3.

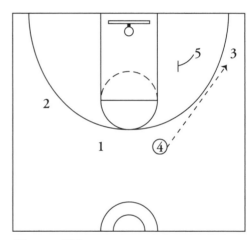

Diagram 226   *Diagram 227*

Player 4's second look is to player 1 cutting backdoor. The timing of this action is crucial. Player 1 will wait for player 2 to cut toward him, as this movement occupies the defender in this area. If player 1 is open, it will be around the foul-line area.

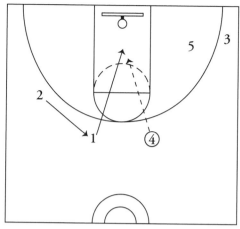

Diagram 228

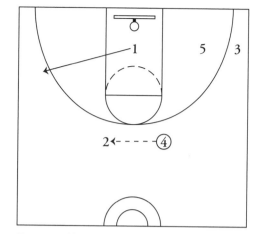

Diagram 229

If player 1 is not open on his backdoor cut, then the ball is to be reversed. As soon as player 1 gets the reversal pass, player 5 will dive to the pinch post looking for the ball. He is also looking to leg whip his defender and slide down the lane line looking for a post feed. Player 5 can also skip the ball across the court.

Diagram 230

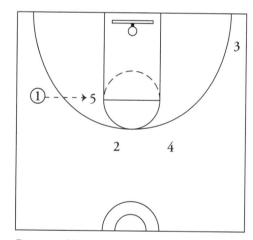

Diagram 231

If player 5 doesn't receive the ball at the pinch post, player 1 will reverse the ball back around to player 4. Player 4 will dribble over toward player 3. This action keys player 5 to cut to the vacant guard spot.

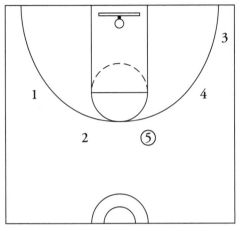

Diagram 232

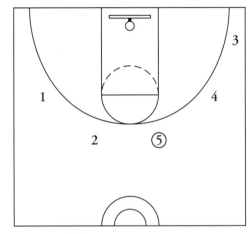

Diagram 233

As soon as player 5 catches the ball, player 1 will set a flare screen for player 2. Player 5 looks to make a pass to player 2.

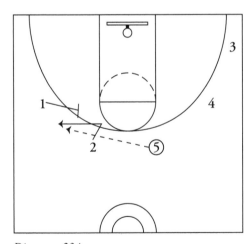

Diagram 234

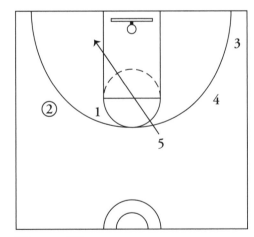

Diagram 235

The diagrams on the next page show how the offense continues from this point.

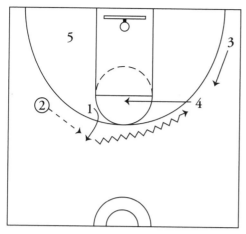

Diagram 236: Player 1 pops up, player 4 to middle.

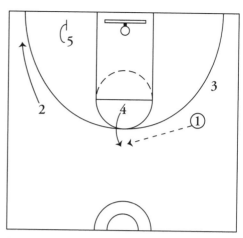

Diagram 237: Player 1 to player 4

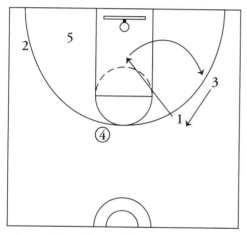

Diagram 238: Player 1 backdoors, player 3 cuts up.

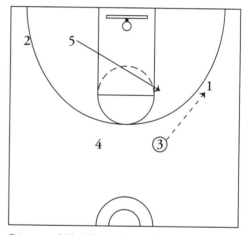

Diagram 239: Player 3 to player 1, player 5 cuts to pinch.

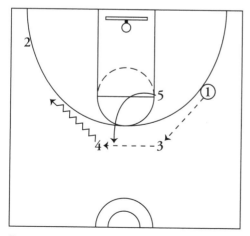

Diagram 240: Player 3 to player 4

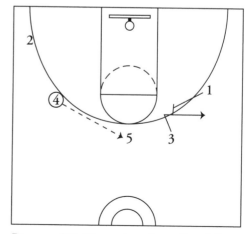

Diagram 241:Player 4 to player 5 and flare action

Princeton Offense Chart

Skill	Dates Covered				
Entries					
G-F Pass					
Push					
Sweep					
Circle					
Samford					
Weakside					
Phases					
Post Feed/Elbow Screen					
Straight Cut					
Backdoor Cut					
Drift					
Three-Point Shot					
Pen & Kick					
Samford					
Forward Dribble					
Second Cutter Read					
Bump up to G Spot					
Screen Down for Post					
Sweep					
Backscreen					
Pinch Post					
Point Screen Away					
Wave					
Under					
Over					
Away					
Reads					
Guarded Closely: Backdoor					
Guarded Loosely: Sweep					
Weak-side Flares					
Sets					
One Guard					
Double					
Invert					
South					
Clone					
Wisconsin					
Purple					
Chin Offense					
Drift/Post Cut					
High Post Feed to W-S Flare					
Clone (G-P)					

Offensive Practice Plan Chart

I. Warm-up drills

    A. Circle and two-spot shooting

    B. Two-ball routine: alternate and rhythm

    C. Change of direction ball-handling routine

        1. Crossover

        2. V-dribble

        3. Behind the back

        4. Between legs

        5. Roll dribble

        6. A.R.C.O.

    D. Joe Scott lay-ups

    E. Partner no travel

    F. Three-man weave to 2-on-1/five-man weave to 3-on-2

    G. Two-man weave

    H. Outlet passing

    I. Three-man push to shots to 3-on-3

II. Guard and forward breakdown drills:

    A. Full-court guard to forward lay-ups

    B. Dribble grinder (most days)

    C. Drift passing and shooting (every day)

        1. Cut, catch and shoot the three

        2. Cut, catch, rip through and pull up

        3. Cut, catch, shot fake and drive in lay-up

        4. Cut, catch, shot fake and pull up

        5. C dribbles at cutter = backdoor cut

        6. Pinch feed to P.S.A. to pop back shot

D. Guard post moves (every day)

    1. Mikan's

    2. Drop steps

    3. Up and unders

    4. Driving hooks

E. Three-man flare shooting.

F. Three-line forward dribble (stress timing).

G. Baseline to free-throw line A.R.C.O.

H. Full-court one-on-one game.

I. Two-side skeleton Iowa entry.

J. 4-on-4 Iowa entry.

K. Two-side skeleton G-F pass and cut-throughs.

L. 4-on-4 entry pass.

    1. V-cut to elbow area and pass

    2. Push

M. Harvard 3-on-3.

N. Get out of trap routine (use some daily).

    1. Havlicek drill

    2. 1-on-2 full-court

    3. 2-on-3 full-court

    4. 4-on-5 box trap drill

    5. 4-on-4/3-on-3 full-court no dribble

O. 20 pass open post without dribble (often).

III. Post Player Breakdown Drills

A. Full-court post sprint-outs.

B. Catch/chin/look—check.

C. 1-on-0 post moves and 1-on-1.

    1. Mikans

    2. Drop steps

      3. Face-ups

      4. Up and under

      5. Driving hooks

      6. Board put-ins

   D. 2-on-2 high-low passing and finishing

   E. Post double down to kick-outs

IV. Team Passing Drills

   A. Two-line stationary

   B. 30 passes/open post drill/no dribble

   C. 3-on-0 perfect pos. game. 25 passes to 3-on-3

V. Fast Break Package/Transition Defense

   A. 2-on-1 bust out

   B. 3-on-2 secondary

   C. 4-on-3 post sprint out

   D. 5-on-5 circle break to secondary

VI. Team Shooting Drills

   A. Two-ball-three-men, first team to 15

   B. Three-man forward dribble to high-low feed

   C. Three-man flare, first team to 15

   D. Three-man forward dribble, first team to 15

      1. C at read spot

      2. C fouling under hoop

   E. 4-man forward dribble with point

      1. C at read spot

      2. C fouling under hoop

   F. Elbow screen completeness

   G. Chin completeness

   H. Post kick-out, first team to 15

I. Wrong way close out shooting, shot fakes

J. Free-throw shooting

    1. Oak Hill free throws

    2. Don Meyer free-throw game

        a. Shoot two in a row

        b. Miss first, must swish second

        c. Make first, must make second

        d. Fail=20 box slides

    3. Team 70% game

        a. Each player shoots on free throw

        b. Team has to make _____

        c. Fail=monster

VII. 3-on-3 Games

A. Post feed to elbow screen.

B. Pinch post to point, to pinch, with wide side wing.

C. Forward dribble.

D. High post phase game (2 posts and 1 guard)

E. Wave action (P.S.A. and pop back and under)

VIII. Team Offense

A. Low post/elbow coverage

    1. Post feed, elbow screen

    2. Forward-guard pass to pinch action

        a. High-low

        b. To pop for pick and roll

    3. Forward-guard pass for drift action

        a. Post feed

        b. Drift

            aa. Shot/drive

            bb. Kick out for reversal

4. Forward dribble

    a. Wing backdoors=high-low

    b. Wing high cuts=pass to post

B. High post phase.

    1. Strong-side cut entry

    2. Posts screen and seal for each other

C. Chin

    1. Running "Jersey" on all UCLA action

    2. Direct pass to post=clone

D. Sets/entries into offense.

E. Zone secondary: Wayne

F. South Carolina, cutter and sets vs. 2-3

G. Zone and man press breaks (add Florida)

H. Xavier and Caston vs. half-court traps

Since 1966 no organization has had a bigger impact on basketball. Five-Star Basketball camps have had more graduates playing college or pro ball than any other organization in the sport. To eat, breathe and live basketball, Five-Star camps are the only place to be! Other popular books from the Five-Star Basketball camps include *Five-Star Girls' Basketball Drills, 2nd Ed.*, *Five-Star Basketball Presents My Favorite Moves: Making the Big Plays* and *Five-Star Basketball Presents My Favorite Moves: Shooting Like the Stars*.

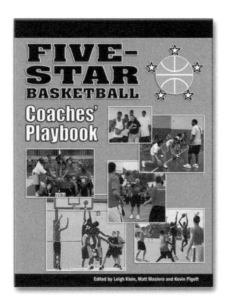

Five-Star Basketball Coaches' Playbook

Edited by Leigh Klein and Matt Masiero

Inside find a variety of the best plays from the coaches who have helped make Five-Star Basketball one of the most respected basketball camps in the world. This collection of plays is so versatile you will find it an indispensable tool, whether you are coaching youth league, high school or college ball.

Coaches who have contributed to this volume include:

Scott Bogumil, Libertyville High School

Mike Brey, University of Notre Dame

John Calipari, University of Memphis

Fran Fraschilla, ESPN

Mike Krzyzewski, Duke University

More than 120 Five-Star campers have played at least one game in the NBA, including the following: Michael Jordan, Jerry Stackhouse, Stevie Francis, Vince Carter, Sam Cassell, Zach Randolph, Rasheed Wallace, Jamal Mashburn, Alonzo Mourning, Grant Hill, Stephon Marbury, Isiah Thomas, Patrick Ewing, Moses Malone and Lebron James.

ISBN-13: 9781930546714 • $18.95 • 256 pages • photos & diagrams • trade paper

Five-Star Basket-ball Coaches' Playbook, Vol. 2

Edited by Leigh Klein and Matt Masiero

The follow-up volume to the popular 2004 playbook, *Five-Star Basketball Coaches' Playbook* includes new plays from even more coaches who have made Five-Star Basketball camps the premier basketball training ground in the country. This volume also includes a section on scouting.

Contributors include:

Tom Penders, University of Houston

Mike Brey, University of Notre Dame

Jay John, Oregon State University

Pete Cinella, American International College

Marsha Sharp, Texas Tech University

ISBN-13: 9781930546806 • $18.95 • 280 pages • photos & diagrams • trade paper

Equilibrium Books are available from bookstores nation-wide or by ordering direct from Cardinal Publishers Group: www.cardinalpub.com.